The Day the Music Died

A poetry collection

Ruthe Wink

Photography by Katie Mlinek

Copyright © 2017 by Ruthe Wink

All rights reserved. No part of this publication may be reproduced, distributed, or transmitted in any form or by any means, including photocopying, recording, or other electronic or mechanical methods, without the prior written permission of the publisher, except in the case of brief quotations embodied in critical reviews and certain other noncommercial uses permitted by copyright law. For permission requests, write to the publisher, addressed "Attention: Permissions Coordinator," at the address below.

Ruthe Wink
ruthewink@gmail.com

Dedicated to a hard working man who believed in Rock n Roll

Acknowedgements

Thank you to my mother for your continuing support and love. He's proud of us.

Thank you to my brothers, all of whom stepped up and set the standard for what men ought to be.

Thank you to all of my classmates and teachers for the critiques and edits. I needed to hear them.

Thank you to Katie Mlinek and Rebecca Schuman for your photography, modeling, and friendship.

Thank you to the Wink and Cooper family's for all of the warmness and deepest love.

Thank you to my Daddy's friends. None of you had to stick around, but you did. We're forever grateful.

Thank you to Carver Center, especially Rebecca Mlinek and Suzanne Supplee, for giving me this platform and your acceptance.

Thank you to Robert Wink Sr. for being the best thing a man could be, a father.

We'll all be equal under the grass, and God's got a heaven for country trash.

-Johnny Cash

Six foot six he stood on the ground, he weighed two hundred and thirty-five pounds, but I saw that giant of a man brought down to his knees by love.

-Johnny Cash

Contents

1. A Warning
2. Red-Neck Vocals
3. American Dreams and Broken Shirt Seams
4. Anatomy by Music
5. Park Bench
6. Inheritance
7. Rain like wet hugs
8. Got Them
9. Shaking Imaginations
10. Father Fox
11. Public Places
12. Warmer
13. Arbutus Boys
14. Gazing
15. Shelter
16. Dread and Death
17. When will they take my balloon away
18. Pink Peony Perfume
19. Taken
20. At the End of the Rope
21. Counting
22. Playground Slides and Empty Skies
23. Newer Men
24. Park Bridge
25. Let's be elephants
26. Footsteps
27. IReligion
28. Angels come with the rain
29. Shadow

30. Here with Me
31. Time has been Forgiving
32. Who
33. More Than Decomp
34. Family sized cheez its
35. Military mustache
36. Courthouse weddings
37. Daddys daddy
38. An Ode
39. Midnight Wanderings
40. Over the Edge
41. Chevy Cruises
42. Tasting Memories
43. Days will not be days
44. Graveyard Geese
45. On Days like Death
46. To Wait Long Enough
47. Robert Wink
48. Fifty Two Ways to Say Goodbye
49. Petco Dumpsters
50. Homes like recycled newspaper
51. Wink Winters
52. White Trees in Heaven
53. Grocery Store Familiars
54. Haunted House
55. Genes come half way split ya know
56. Daddy Do I
57. The Nightmare of a Dream
58. Forest
59. When there are none left to count
60. Maes house is for sale
61. Heaven has glass flooring
62. Like It's Been Awhile

63. Springtime in Arbutus
64. Daddy's Girl

A Poetry Collection

Red-Neck Vocals

Last night I sang to the cd we bought
in the old record store
that smelled like cat piss and leather.
I went by early this morning to tell the goatee man
that you died
and not to worry about your big beer belly filling up his aisles
no more.

The Day the Music Died

                American Dreams and Broken Shirt Seams
I'd rather make butter and grape jelly sandwiches
for lunch and squish in cool mud
on a warm day and let my knees breath
through the holes in my jeans
and take quick cold showers by candlelight because
at least it the dark, there is plenty of room
to dream.

Anatomy by Music

If you let that warm ribbon
rest easy on your bones,
that deep drum twitch
your pinky toes,
that big bass soften
your backbones,
you will know
Rock n Roll.

The Day the Music Died

                                          Inheritance
You left me with a two cent stereo
that sings cheap rhymes to any tune
I do no want,
with transmission blown engines
20 years past oil checks
and giant holes in the walls
that put out welcome mats for floods.
You left me without telling me
I'd have to walk myself down the aisle,
without telling me
how to hot glue this house back together.
You left me with
out.

A Poetry Collection

The Day the Music Died

                        Rain like Wet Hugs

These
thousand
water
droplets
weigh down
my clothes my
skin running down
my cheeks like non-swiped
tears I'm swimming in the black
of this night with lightning
like lightning bugs.
This is what
it's like to be
surrounded.

Got Them

She stands next to me with her
dead flat hair and those
smeared candy lips
and plants her feet.
You're alone, she says. *alone.*
and a crowd gathers at her toes.

I got my momma's long legs, I say
and my daddy's blue eyes. Got his nose, too.

You're alone, she says. *alone.*
and she sucks in her gut.

I got my daddy's yellow teeth, I say
and my grandmomma's chin. Got her red hair, too.
and a crowd gathers at my toes,
and they're shining white.
I ain't alone, I say. *I ain't*

The Day the Music Died

                                        Shaking Imaginations
My hands shake and sometimes I imagine
if I were to put a pen
in my shaking hands, maybe
a message from you would scratch itself
out, and we would be together.
Sometimes, I imagine
if I did not shake at all, maybe
that would be the worst thing
imaginable.

Father Fox

A small brown fox crosses the way
tips his hat
and goes home to the bushes.
First he kisses his wife,
a side mouthed kind of kiss,
with his fox mustache tickling her cheek.
Then he hugs his little cubs
all five of them
in his small fox arms.
He had worked a double shift
managing their neighbeavers
and their oh so fragile dams.
But he brought home some sticks
one for each pup, and a leaf
for his wife.
Mrs. Fox places this one on her dresser
with all of the rest
and thanks her husband
for working so foxing hard.

The Day the Music Died

                                              Public Places
You float above me standing with a
left hip jutted and your
arms crossed loosely, you've got that
military mustache and your
leather jacket from
thirty pounds ago and I know
that others can't see you and daddy I
wish you were real again.

Warmer

You
are the solid
stroke
of a bluesman's
guitar
echoing
shameless
hanging
onto that black
empty
space
and making it feel
warmer.

The Day the Music Died

                                        Arbutus Boys
My daddy got five friends that he
left to me they got
yellow plagued teeth and
glossy blue eyes and
big leather jackets like daddys.
My daddy was the leader he could
flick a dart so good you
never saw it comin he could
swallow more pints and
look better while doing it.
These friends of his they got
no one now they got
no one like I got
no one so I guess we
gonna have each other now.

Shelter

The wind burns
my hunched white shoulders
and I shudder
to the rhythm of the rain.
I wish again
for your big red back
and those black
blue eyes
to take me away
up
past the stars.

The Day the Music Died

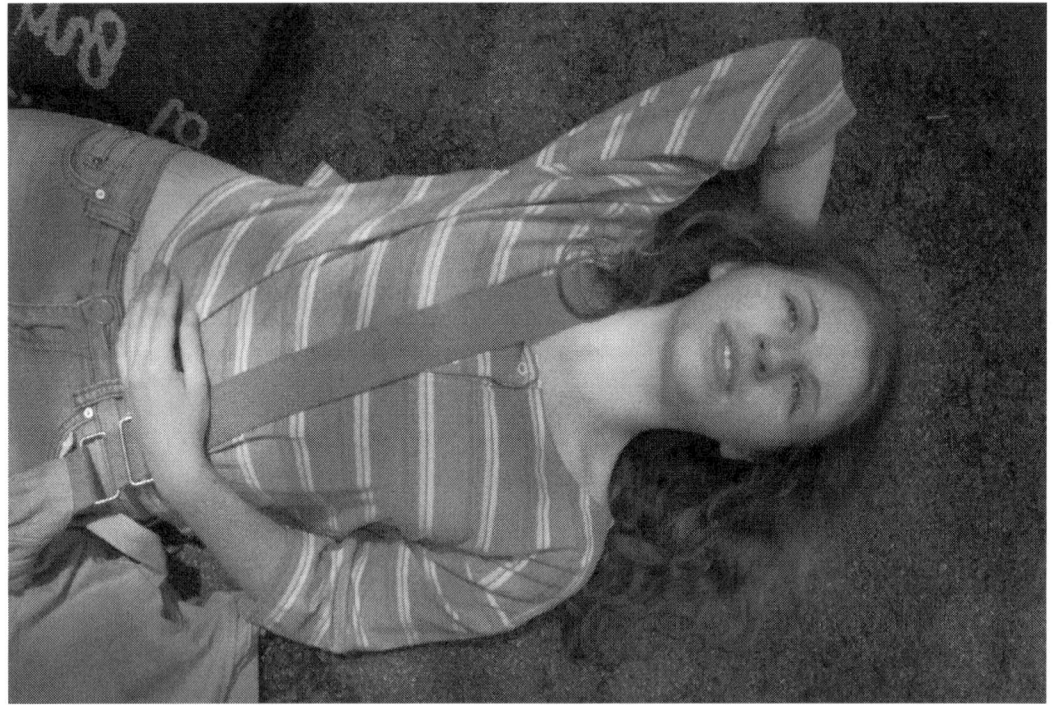

Dread and Death

I dread the day
when 60's leather
and black oil stains
are just that.
When Bob Dylan
is just a man
and Bud Light
just a beer.
I dread the day
I forget your face
in these things
on that day,
you will truly be dead,
leather just leather
cigarettes just cigarettes
Robert Wink just Robert Wink.
I dread the day
that you will leave me
for the second
and final time.
I dread that day
I dread it worse than death.

The Day the Music Died

      When Will They Take My Balloon Away
When will they take my balloon away?
I've stood here
with that thin white string
for months
letting the rain smack
my face, staring
out into those black
clouds. I've stood here
with my tall
red balloon
facing the sunset
and hoping that one dry day
your hands would replace
this string
and your heart
this balloon.

Pink Peony Perfume

Today,
Momma cleaned
the bathroom
for the first time
since you left.
She covered it in pink,
peony perfume that stung
my eyes and nose.
She threw away
your toothbrush,
because Daddy,
you don't need it.
Now every room
was done and clean.
Clean of things of you
and yours.

The Day the Music Died

Taken

God,
you've taken my daddy
up to those fat
white clouds,
and your long golden
gates.
You've taken him
to a world without jobs
or water damage
or alcoholism.
God,
you've taken my daddy.
Make him an angel.
Give him wings,
so I can have my daddy
back again.

At the End of the Rope

,
he held on
hands bleeding from open blisters
and open palms.
His teeth were fighting with strings
and losing. Problems
Neck problems
Back problems
Heart problems
Knee problems
Problems
Problems
Problems
Problems
Problems
I hear there aren't any ropes in heaven.

The Day the Music Died

Counting

How many man
made bricks
thick with red
will it take
to hide me
from the gray
of the world
How long
until these fat
stump blocks
block out
the raw throat
screaming
How many
dark filled
days
will it take
for me to break
like you broke
How many
hushed
night prayers
does it take
to get into heaven

Playground Slides and Empty Skies

I sit and let the sunburned slide stick
to my thighs, waiting til my nicotine protector
emerges from the gates he's locked behind. The sun is
going down and the moon is coming up and
I'm too scared to move 'cause I'm
worried I won't be able to. So I sit. A decade more
upon the piss yellow slide. The children
try to climb around me. *Move. Move.*
I'm waiting. I say.
You're dying. They say. *You'll die waiting.*

The Day the Music Died

Newer Men

She's got a new man
now. I hear
he doesn't smoke and
he brushes his teeth.
I hear he's not scared
of heights or bad jazz
bands. I hear he has tan skin
and a tight tummy.
I hear he doesn't have blue
eyes or fluffy man slippers.
I hear he doesn't like football
or busy Baltimore streets.
I hear we've got a new man
now. But he'll never
be my daddy.

Let's be Elephants

If I held on
to your skinny gray
tail, would you lead me over
the dead skin deserts of Botswana
the rushed waterfalls of Zimbabwe and
the tight tree trunks of the Congo.
If I held on
with my skinnier,
grayer trunk, would you lead me
back home
to the brickstone buildings
of Baltimore.

The Day the Music Died

                        Footsteps
I spent the day in your flat grass footsteps
following them like the
red black lines of a
treasure map.

The Day the Music Died

                        iReligion

I've googled heaven
and how to get there,
Siri doesn't know
or won't tell me.
Momma has an app
to tell us where
your phone is,
Verizon says
you're unavailable.
I don't think
Smartphones
know what God is.
I don't think
I do.

Angels Come with the Rain

Angels come with the rain
and whisper
in raindrops
on windowsills
Angels come with the rain
and take away
those in their beds
with a gust of wind.
Angels come with the rain
and leave trails
of lightning
up past
the clouds
to come again.

The Day the Music Died

Here with Me

I saw you sitting there
resting
on the corner of my bed
I saw you nod to me
nod away
those bad black dreams

A Poetry Collection

The Day the Music Died

                               Time has been Forgiving
Yellow days have passed me by
and I,
I noticed for the first time
that the world has yet to die.

Die like you and die like me
fleeing
from this world with not seeing, a
goodbye to one's own being

Nature, with death and life so
wovn
might kiss me dearly,
then passover.

Who

Who will tell me how love
flies from bluebird to nesting dove
why angels live so high above

Who will tell me these I need
to live a life blind from greed
Who will? Who will love me

The Day the Music Died

                        More than Decomp

I have to believe in god
so that you're not just growing holes
in the form of maggot homes
and your blue eyes that look like mine
aren't just shrinking and sagging and scrambling
like something savory
for the worms. I have to believe in God
so that I can wake up
with my dry throw up throat
and weird sweaty body
everyday because there's something bearable
about your big beer belly floating
over me, protecting me
from your six feet under.

Family Sized Cheez-Its

At 5am they sip at their iced coffees and steaming teas
and give half assed hugs in between bites
of their fruit salad,
while i eat my Cheez-its. You loved Cheez-its,
like really fucking loved those fake cheese things
that leave your throat dry
and smelling like that weird cheese taste.
They were your dinner side salad, your dipping
soup crackers, your late night fat attack,
so I've been penciling them into my schedule
like breathes to take. If nothing else,
I hope this makes you proud.

The Day the Music Died

Military Mustache

We buried you in that
military mustache
from 18,
combed and cut
before the corner
of your lips, the one
that tickled my cheek and twitched
around when you thought
daddy thoughts. They say
hair is the last thing to go,
and I can see you now, nothin
but bone and that old
military mustache.

Courthouse Weddings

You and momma and nothin' to your name cept love
so you married in a courthouse with your best button up and her
old blue dress and y'all had the time so you threw a party
with cheap beer and fat balloons and coloring books for me and the boys.
Some years later momma looked at me and said now
you find a man who don't care about big white weddings
or how many kids you got 'cause that'll be the man
you'll die with and momma was kinda right 'cause you died
in her bed all nice and warm wearing nothin' but that ring
and your holy underwear.

The Day the Music Died

Daddy's Daddy

Your daddy was a man who believed
in things like belt bruises and free-for-all
spaghetti dinners, cause that was more
than what his daddy
gave him. Daddy's are simple men,
believing in things like holy
underwear and spit and mud
and clean plate clubs and two pound
meatballs. My daddy was a simple man.
He believed in things like dinner cigarettes
and pre ice-cream ice-cream,
things like family tattoos on
forearms and mustache kisses
on cheeks. Daddys believe in these things
cause their daddy did
and it was simpler that way.

An Ode

to single brick houses
with brick stairs
brick beds
brick walls
fingertips
cut from
fingers like brick
homes standing
between two
parking lots.

The Day the Music Died

Midnight Wanderings
I remember the night that you drunk peed
on my bedroom floor
because it was dark and I guess
my room smelled like pee
anyway. I put a towel on it to stop it from leaking
between the cracks of the hardwood
and called it a night,
plopping down into bed and falling asleep
like a drunk man.

Chevy Cruises

Because we sat, sweat sticking us
to seats for hours, because
there was always change for ice cream
pit stops, because your hands
were the only hands
the steering wheel knew,
and because there was nothing
more calming than a cruise,
I will keep
my daddy's car.

The Day the Music Died

Tasting Memories

Sweet cherry syrup memories
fade
into whispers
so we stick out our tongues
to catch the snow.

The Day the Music Died

Days will not be days
on days like this so taken.
A man turns into man
on the day you were so taken

Graveyard Geese

A Mister Goose and a Misses Goose
gathered round a graveyard
reading names and giving gifts
with little goose signed cards.

"Say hello, Mrs. Goose,"
the mister sir had said.
Say hello to all those buried
before we too, are dead."

The lady bird did turn round
and stare him in the eye,
"Say no more to me, dear Goose,
I know all dead must rise."

And stepping to her bird mans car
the mistress then called out,
"It's getting late and I grow tired,
of your words I am in doubt.

Those birds are empty,
yet their bodies you do gift.
On them you waste your cent but me,
you dare not spend a fifth."

"You may believe in God, my girl,
you may believe in none,
but shun me not for showing care
before our times begun."

The Day the Music Died

                                      On days
like death
I don't believe in Rock n Roll
or short men with long hair
or 99 cent Hallmark cards
or sterile Band-Aids
or experienced doctors
or long Chevy rides
or grass seed
or how-to books
or 9-5 jobs
or black grease
like death.

The Day the Music Died

To Wait Long Enough

For months we waited
with our words caught
in our throats
and our eyes stuck
on the big brass door,
for you to come strolling
through it, to put your
hand in your side and
say It's me, I'm back.
And I'd cry and momma'd
cry and Bear would be still
but happy
and we'd run to the basement
to watch Mash and I'd
sit between you and momma
with our popcorn fingers and
popcorn teeth and it'd be this way
for forever. But the hours get longer
and the days stretch by like
God's pulling them apart
and it's been nearly two
years and millions of seconds
and even though we don't wait
like dogs at the door
anymore we all still jump
at the sound of metal keys
in metal locks and get disappointed
when it's just each other
and not the man who used
to be my daddy.

A Poetry Collection

The Day the Music Died

                                          Robert Wink

Raised by red-necked rednecks
Our father grew up fast and grew up mean.
Born with raw meat sandwiches already in his bloodstream
Exhaled by God himself to
Return at the ripe age of 52.
To heaven and hell and back again
We watched him fly like comets
Inching through the sky
Never to come home,
Knowing maybe he was too much for us anyway.

A Poetry Collection

Fifty Two Ways to Say Goodbye

1. Spit fresh spit into each other's hands; shake.
2. Type up a letter. Deliver that letter.
3. Type up a letter. Cry. Rip it up. Hug Instead.
4. Hug.
5. Find a field. Yell across it.
6. Bake them a cake, get fancy with the lettering.
7. Stuff your face with cake beforehand so you're too full to cry.
8. Write a message on the ceiling fan.
9. Jump rope in morse code.
10. Drink a beer. Slur your way through it.
11. Drink ten beers, regret it, drink ten more. Forget.
12. Bring a boombox for tension.
13. Use a song.
14. Stare.
15. Throw away your matching underwear.
16. Re-plumb the house in the shape of waving hands.
17. Wave from across a field.
18. Carve out a pumpkin. Aim. Fire.
19. Give back that necklace.
20. Cover them in stickers. Run.
21. Put your finger up and shhhhh. Back away. Then run.
22. Give them a bad haircut.
23. Turn off the lights. Escape.
24. Learn how to ninja. Ninja away.
25. Draw a picture of you and someone else. Give it to them.
26. Run.
27. Give them a kite during a lightning storm.
28. Uninstall Snapchat.
29. Play tag and just leave.
30. Play

The Day the Music Died

31. Tag
32. And
33. Just
34. Leave
35. Make them a sad poster.
36. Buy airtime during the superbowl. Wave for 15 seconds.
37. Make them a happy poster.
38. Run away in slow motion.
39. Tell them you love them in an inappropriate situation .
40. Crash their computer.
41. Wear really bad makeup to dinner.
42. Throw up dinner.
43. Buy them an airline ticket.
44. Buy them a train ticket.
45. Buy them a bus ticket.
46. Buy them a submarine.
47. Join the military.
48. Start another war with Iraq.
49. Take them to the zoo and jump in the lion's den.
50. Learn sign language. Sign goodbye.
51. Mouth it to them from across a field.
52. Don't

Petco Dumpsters

Uncle Joe did the uncle thing
and went to a bar
to pick up a cat.
We called him patches cuz he was white
with black spots
and black dots
from flees.
He got fat like Uncle Joe
and you said
Joe had his work ethic. None.
Patches died in the corner
of the basement that leaks and puddles
when it rains. You and Joe threw
his big fat cat body into the Petco dumpster
across the way,
and told me you buried him
in the park we used to go to.
That was the only thing Joe
ever gave me.

The Day the Music Died

Homes Like Recycled Newspaper

With blindfolded eyes
tissue tearing into corneas
like shower curtains
whispering goodbye
to the home you bought us
the bookshelves you built
and the flooring you put in
drunk one night,
with my brothers as bartenders
and tool boxes.
Hot glueing that fabric to my eyes
I walk
to Iowa, barefoot and still
whispering.

Wink Winters

Momma grew up in the snow and
daddy grew up poor so
our heat is never on.
We used to pile blankets
on ourselves like
mini snow mounds and
our arms would get stuck so
you'd have to pile for us.
More daddy more and
soon we're stuffed like turkeys or
like momma's sweet apple pie
warm in all the right ways.

The Day the Music Died

                                              White trees in heaven
white bark like white clouds
smooth for the tongue
easy on the hips.
White trees in heaven
to see from my daddy's window
and thank the stars for.

Grocery Store Familiars

I shoulder-bumped a guy
in the bargain aisle in Giant,
he was a cigarette ashtray
the kind that is used through winter
cuz freezing is better than quitting.
His skin was a big brown worker mans jacket
and his toes
were thick warehouse boots. He was about 20
years younger
than you, daddy,
but God,
how smokers smell the same in winter.

The Day the Music Died

Haunted House

Daddy is a ghost
who haunts our house with
Pink Floyd whisperings and disappearing
chicken wings. Some days I think
he's our dog, when he looks at me
with soft human eyes and finds
me in a corner when I'm scared at night.
We feed the dog three times a day now,
otherwise dad pees on the floor.
But when Duke is dead
and we're moved out, I just pray
for whoever moves in, and I hope
they like Rock n Roll.

Genes Come Split Half Way Ya Know
because you played when you were young
barely there leather leather mitts and
cotton stitched leather shoes,
Andrew has to
too. But brother Bear
doesn't have that baseball gene you
gotta know by now his
tempers too hot like that
alligator hot sauce
and his mind can't stay like a
never ending ride and, Daddy,
he just ain't you

The Day the Music Died

                              Daddy do I
ask permission to drink Cokes in strangers cars or sip away
do I pay to park here or drive til I find a spot
do I give momma the better present on Mother's Day or her birthday
do I need that extra screw or will the door stay on just fine
do I use paper towels to clean the Chevy tires or a the special red rag
do I keep those old Bluejay baseball cards or toss em
do I talk to the bagger at Giant or let him do his work
do I have to print out my resume on white paper or do managers like blue
do I let a man pay for my dinner or should I offer
do I move to Iowa with momma or
do I stay with you

The Nightmare of a Dream

How wrong it is to wish
one parent for the other
but the mind cannot help but think
of one's life with another.

Had mother died instead of father,
the law so swift could fall
or freedom in the form of trust
could rain upon them all.

How sweet it is to think
of a life that could have been
but love your loved in today
like dreams in form of kin.

The Day the Music Died

When There Are None Left to be Counted

Turn off the lights and think about
rain drop races on car windows and hot
hot chocolate resting in tummies on white
snow days and small birds in big flocks
that seem to follow the wind and fat
cats tucked into themselves asleep
on fleece blankets

The Day the Music Died

       Mae's House is for Sale
Jenny thinks the neighbors
are gonna be rednecks. Momma thinks
they'll be black. Bear thinks gays.
I just hope they like
daddy's car coughing
out oil in the early morning
and Bob Dylan from the window
late at night.

Heaven Has Glass Flooring

I think I'll cry at my graduation,
at that little red check at the top of the list
of my life you'd miss.
But I think I'll laugh right after
at the sight of you proud of me
graduating from art school
of all things.
You can't hide from me old man
I see you crying too

The Day the Music Died

                            Like It's Been Awhile

For months we been trying
to get that grass growing green
over dad. Kentucky Bluegrass
and fertilizer don't work it's time
that covers dirt.
For months we been trying
to give that old man some damn
grass and now that it's here
it's like a seal on the space
between this world
and the next.

Springtime in Arbutus

In the spring,
the yellow daffodils in our
small, side house garden,
fell open against the long, upperclass grass
that rolled down the hill
from our neighbors. Daddy wasn't
allowed to tame our
backyard jungle, with white flower
weeds and wet morning dew,
until Easter. Momma'd hide
our dollar store jewels
in the roots of our yard
and sip and the tip
of her fading coffee mug, watching
our pajamaed feet search and search
for the eggs that looked like
spring flowers.

The Day the Music Died

                          Daddy's Girl

I got my daddy's fat tongued
sailors mouth with its
red hot temper like them
hot sand days and nothin'
to cool it down with.
I got my daddy's
brick built head with its
big leaking creaks like an
empty jailmans cell and nothin'
to fill it up with.

Made in the USA
Middletown, DE
05 May 2017